SCRAPPY JACK: 100 YEARS OF HARDSHIP, LAUGHTER, AND RECYCLING
© MIDTOWN PRESS, 2023

ISBN 978-1-988242-52-1 (PRINT)
ISBN 978-1-988242-53-8 (EPUB)

LEGAL DEPOSIT: 4TH QUARTER 2023
PRINTED IN CHINA BY WKT COMPANY LIMITED

EDITOR: LOUIS ANCTIL
ASSISTANT: DANIEL ANCTIL
LAYOUT AND PRODUCTION: KEN STEACY

LIBRARY AND ARCHIVES CANADA CATALOGUING IN PUBLICATION

TITLE: SCRAPPY JACK: 100 YEARS OF HARDSHIP, LAUGHTER, AND RECYCLING BY JOAN STEACY.
OTHER TITLES: SO, THAT'S THAT! NAMES: STEACY, JOAN, AUTHOR/ILLUSTRATOR.
DESCRIPTION: PREVIOUSLY PUBLISHED UNDER THE TITLE: SO, THAT'S THAT!
IDENTIFIERS: CANADIANA (PRINT) 20230529356 | CANADIANA (EBOOK) 20230529410
ISBN 9781988242521 (HARDCOVER) ISBN 9781988242553B (EPUB)
SUBJECTS: LCSH: THORNBORROW, JACK -- JUVENILE LITERATURE.
| LCSH: SCRAP METAL INDUSTRY--CANADA--EMPLOYEES--BIOGRAPHY--JUVENILE LITERATURE.
| LCGFT: BIOGRAPHIES. | LCGFT: ILLUSTRATED WORKS.
CLASSIFICATION: LCC HD8039.R4582 C37 2023 | DDC J331.7/616284092--DC23

Midtown Press

WWW.MIDTOWNPRESS.CA

SCRAPPY JACK

100 YEARS OF HARDSHIP, LAUGHTER, AND RECYCLING

by JOAN STEACY

MY FATHER'S NAME WAS JACK, AND LATER IN HIS LIFE HE WAS CALLED 'SCRAPPY JACK'. HE WAS BORN IN LONDON, ENGLAND IN 1906 TO A MIDDLE-CLASS FAMILY, AND WOULD LIVE TO BE 100 YEARS OLD!

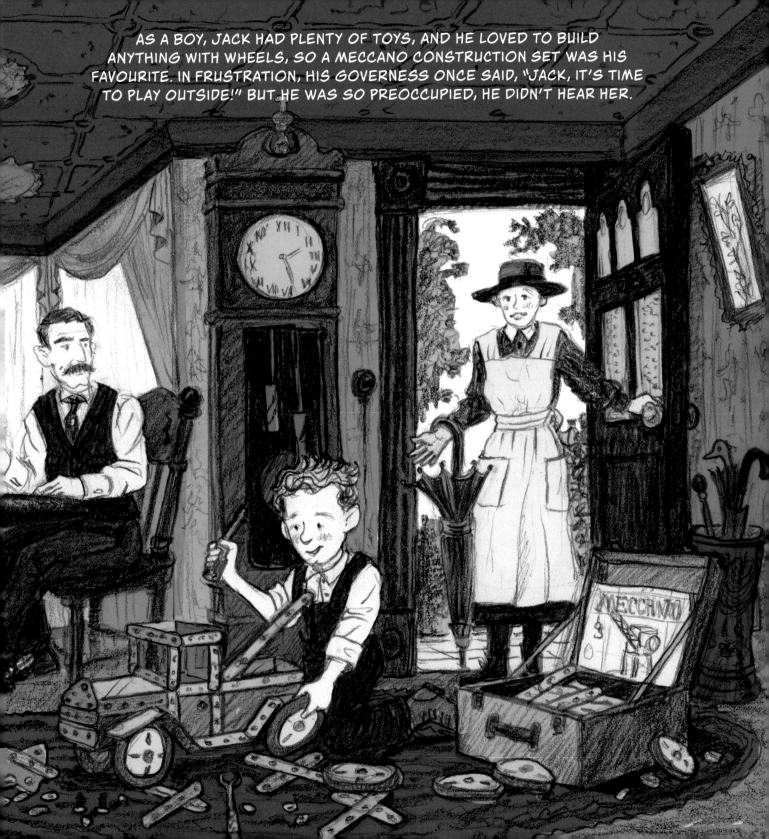

AS A BOY, JACK HAD PLENTY OF TOYS, AND HE LOVED TO BUILD ANYTHING WITH WHEELS, SO A MECCANO CONSTRUCTION SET WAS HIS FAVOURITE. IN FRUSTRATION, HIS GOVERNESS ONCE SAID, "JACK, IT'S TIME TO PLAY OUTSIDE!" BUT HE WAS SO PREOCCUPIED, HE DIDN'T HEAR HER.

WHEN JACK WAS SIX, HIS FATHER'S BUSINESS FAILED AND HIS
PARENTS COULDN'T AFFORD TO BUY ANY MORE TOYS FOR HIM OR
FOR HIS TWO BROTHERS. HIS FATHER WANTED HIM TO BE HAPPY, AND
SAID EXCITEDLY, "WE'RE ALL GOING ON AN ADVENTURE - IN A BIG
STEAMBOAT, TO ANOTHER LAND!" JACK JUMPED FOR JOY.

LIKE MANY BRITISH FAMILIES AT THE TIME, JACK'S PARENTS DECIDED TO START THEIR NEW LIFE IN CANADA. THEY EMIGRATED TO HAMILTON, ONTARIO IN 1912, SIX MONTHS AFTER THE TITANIC SANK. DURING THE VOYAGE JACK'S FATHER ARRANGED A VISIT TO THE ENGINE ROOM. JACK WAS FASCINATED BY THE ENORMOUS PISTONS, FLYWHEELS, AND GEARS, WHICH REMINDED HIM OF HIS MECCANO SET... ONLY MUCH BIGGER!

HAMILTON WAS AN INDUSTRIAL TOWN, AND THE BAD SMELL OF
THE STEEL MILLS WAS JUST A PART OF THE DAY-TO-DAY STRUGGLE
TO SURVIVE THAT THE FAMILY HAD TO LEARN TO LIVE WITH.

ON AN ERRAND WITH HIS FATHER ONE FREEZING DAY, JACK SAW
A MECCANO SET IN THE WINDOW OF EATON'S DEPARTMENT STORE THAT HE
KNEW HE COULDN'T HAVE. INSTEAD, HIS FATHER MADE HIS CHILDREN A SET
OF WOODEN BLOCKS TO STUFF THEIR STOCKINGS AT CHRISTMAS, SO
JACK HAD TO USE HIS IMAGINATION, AND MAKE HIS OWN TOYS.

LIFE IN HAMILTON BECAME EVEN MORE DIFFICULT FOR THE FAMILY
WHEN THE GREAT DEPRESSION LEFT MANY PEOPLE OUT OF WORK. THE
COMFORTABLE LIFE THE FAMILY ONCE ENJOYED IN ENGLAND WAS NOW
A FADING MEMORY, AND JACK'S MOTHER HAD TO LEARN TO DO ALL THE
THINGS THEIR GOVERNESS HAD ONCE DONE.

AS THE FAMILY GREW, FOOD AND CLOTHES BECAME MORE SCARCE,
AND JACK HAD TO SHARE WHAT LITTLE THEY HAD WITH HIS YOUNGER
BROTHERS. THE FAMILY WAS CONSTANTLY ON THE MOVE BECAUSE THE
RENT BECAME MORE AND MORE UNAFFORDABLE, AND SADLY THEY HAD
TO PLACE JACK AND ONE OF HIS BROTHERS IN AN ORPHANAGE.

AT LEAST THERE, THEIR PARENTS THOUGHT THE BOYS
WOULD HAVE PROPER FOOD AND SHELTER.

A FEW PAINFUL YEARS
WENT BY, UNTIL THEIR PARENTS
COULD AFFORD TO TAKE THE
BOYS BACK HOME AGAIN.

AS JACK LATER DESCRIBED
IT, THIS EXPERIENCE OF BEING
'WATERED AND FED' LEFT HIM AND
HIS BROTHER WITH A VERY NEGATIVE
VIEW OF INSTITUTIONS, ESPECIALLY
ONES LIKE SCHOOL.

JACK HAD DIFFICULTY LEARNING TO READ, BUT ONCE HE DID LEARN, HE JUST COULDN'T STOP. HE WAS SO INTERESTED IN BOOKS THAT HE LATER CLAIMED TO HAVE READ EVERY BOOK IN THE HAMILTON LIBRARY.

THE LIBRARIAN COULDN'T BELIEVE
HOW MANY BOOKS HE BORROWED,
BUT SHE JUST KEPT BRINGING HIM
MORE - AND MORE, AND MORE!

JACK WAS TOO YOUNG TO SERVE
DURING WORLD WAR I, BUT WAS
OLD ENOUGH TO WITNESS ITS TRAGIC
IMPACT ON HIS COMMUNITY.

THE RETURNING SOLDIERS MARCHED
IN A PARADE, BUT THE ONES WHO
COULDN'T MARCH WERE LET OFF ON
A PLATFORM HIDDEN FROM THE PUBLIC.
JACK WATCHED IN HORROR AS A YOUNG
SOLDIER WAS CARRIED OFF THE TRAIN IN
A BASKET, THEN PLACED IN A WHEELCHAIR.
HE HAD NO ARMS OR LEGS, BUT STILL
WORE A PROUD SMILE FOR FAITHFULLY
SERVING HIS COUNTRY.

JACK HAD A MISCHIEVOUS SENSE OF HUMOUR, WHICH GREW AS HE BECAME A YOUNG MAN, AND SO DID HIS SENSE OF ADVENTURE, ESPECIALLY WHEN IT CAME TO ANYTHING WITH WHEELS. ONE TIME ON A COLD WINTER NIGHT HE CONVINCED HIS BROTHERS TO TAKE AN OLD FORD OUT FOR A SPIN ON THE FROZEN HAMILTON HARBOUR BAY.

HE REASSURED THEM THAT THE "OPERATOR IS IN CONTROL" AND RACED THE OLD JALOPY AS FAST AS IT COULD GO, THEN SLAMMED ON THE BRAKES! THE CAR SPUN WILDLY ROUND AND ROUND, DID A FEW DONUTS, THEN CAME TO AN ABRUPT STOP WHEN THE WOODEN SPOKES OF ALL FOUR WHEELS COMPLETELY SHEARED OFF! THEIR PREDICAMENT LEFT THEM IN A STATE OF SHOCK AND HYSTERICAL LAUGHTER. THE CAR WAS NOTHING BUT SCRAP NOW, AND THEY ALL KNEW THEY'D HAVE A LOT OF EXPLAINING TO DO, BUT ANY WITNESS WOULD SURELY SAY THAT THE PUNISHMENT FIT THE CRIME. "SO, THAT'S THAT!" AS JACK WOULD SAY.

DURING THE DEPRESSION WORK WAS HARD TO FIND, AND LIKE MANY YOUNG MEN JACK DECIDED TO RIDE THE TRAINS OUT WEST IN SEARCH OF EMPLOYMENT AND ADVENTURE. JACK KNEW THE DIFFERENCE BETWEEN THE HARDWORKING HOBO, AND THE LAZY, FREELOADING BUM. HE QUICKLY LEARNED IMPORTANT SURVIVAL SKILLS TOO, LIKE THE RIGHT AND WRONG WAY OF JUMPING THE TRAIN CARS AS THEY PASSED, WHEN A MISTAKE COULD COST A LIMB - OR A LIFE.

JACK WOULD HOP OFF THE TRAIN TO FIND WORK AT FARMS ALONG THE WAY. CLOTHING WAS SCARCE, AND WITH A BUTTON IN HIS HAND, JACK WOULD ASK A FARMER'S WIFE IF SHE HAD A SHIRT TO SEW THE BUTTON ONTO! CHICKENS OFTEN WENT MISSING FROM FARMS, ONLY TO TURN UP AT THE HOBO'S CAMP, WHICH WAS CALLED THE "JUNGLE." THEY DIDN'T HAVE A POT TO COOK THE CHICKEN, SO THEY COATED IT IN CLAY, AND BUILT A FIRE OVER IT, LIKE AN OVEN. AFTERWARDS THERE WAS NOTHING LEFT BUT "THE BONES AND THE BEAK" AND IT WAS THE BEST CHICKEN HE'D EVER TASTED.

SOME HOBOS DID NOT SURVIVE RIDING ON TOP OF THE TRAIN DURING THE HARSH WINTER, BUT LUCKILY BEFORE LEAVING HAMILTON A FRIEND GAVE JACK A SHEEPSKIN COAT THAT KEPT HIM WARM, AND PROBABLY SAVED HIS LIFE. A KINDLY ENGINEER LET JACK SHOVEL COAL FROM THE TENDER BEHIND THE LOCOMOTIVE, AND YEARS LATER HIS FAVOURITE JOKE WAS, "LAST NIGHT I DREAMED I WAS A LOCOMOTIVE, AND WOKE UP WITH A TENDER BEHIND!"

WORLD WAR II ENDED THE DEPRESSION, AND IN 1939
THE HAMILTON STEEL COMPANIES SUPPLIED THE METAL
TO BUILD THE MACHINERY OF WAR.

MANY WOMEN REPLACED THE MEN WHO HAD
VOLUNTEERED FOR MILITARY SERVICE, BUT JACK WAS
NOT ONE OF THEM. HE LATER RECALLED THAT HE WASN'T
ACCEPTED BECAUSE HE WAS CONSIDERED UNHEALTHY, BUT
DELIGHTED IN TELLING HIS FRIENDS HE WOULD OUTLIVE
ALL OF THOSE WHO WERE ACCEPTED – AND HE DID.

JACK WORKED AT THE WESTINGHOUSE FACTORY IN HAMILTON, WHICH HAD BEEN CONVERTED INTO A MUNITIONS ASSEMBLY LINE.

HE WAS FASCINATED BY HOW THE OLD SCRAP METAL THAT EVERYONE COLLECTED FOR THE WAR EFFORT WAS RECYCLED INTO CANNONS AND ARTILLERY SHELLS. NOTHING WAS THROWN AWAY THAT COULD BE REUSED, AND JACK BECOME MORE AND MORE AWARE OF THE GREAT VALUE OF SCRAP.

AFTER THE WAR, JACK AND HIS WIFE EMILY RAISED FOUR KIDS ON SOME LAND THEY BOUGHT NORTH OF HAMILTON. HE WAS THE LAST PERSON TO GET A SCRAP METAL LICENCE IN ONTARIO, WHICH MADE HIM HAPPY SINCE HE KNEW THERE WAS MONEY TO BE MADE IN "SCRAP". JACK ACCEPTED WHAT PEOPLE CONSIDERED JUNK, BUT TO HIM THE WORD MEANT MONEY IN THE BANK. THAT'S WHEN HE GOT THE NICKNAME 'SCRAPPY JACK'!

SOME PIECES OF METAL COULD
BE BROKEN UP BY POUNDING IT WITH A
SLEDGEHAMMER, BUT FOR THE BIGGER
PIECES HE'D USE DYNAMITE! THIS METHOD
WOULD SOMETIMES RESULT WITH A WHEEL
LANDING IN THE NEIGHBOUR'S FIELD, BUT
LUCKILY NO-ONE EVER GOT HURT.

OUR MOM EMILY PREFERRED TO STAY
IN THE HOUSE WHERE IT WAS SAFE.

GROWING UP, THE SCRAPYARD WAS THE BEST PLAYGROUND FOR US KIDS, WITH LIFE-SIZE CARS AND TRUCKS WE COULD PLAY IN. BUT JACK ALSO EXPECTED US TO WORK IN THE YARD AT TIMES, AND OUR JOB WAS SORTING THE SCRAP METAL TO BE RECYCLED IN HAMILTON.

WE LEARNED THE DIFFERENCE BETWEEN METALS; COPPER
WAS REDDISH AND TURNED GREEN WHEN IT GOT OLD, ALUMINUM
WAS LIGHT GREY AND LIGHT AS A FEATHER, BRASS WAS BRIGHT
YELLOW IF YOU POLISHED IT, AND IRON WOULD RUST TO RED. BUT IRON
WAS TOO HEAVY TO PICK UP, SO JACK WOULD DO THE HEAVY LIFTING,
SINCE HE WAS STRONG - LIKE IRON MAN!

JACK NEEDED
A WAY OF MOVING
AND STACKING THE
CARS, SO HE BUILT THE
'BOOMTRUCK' OUT OF
SCRAP VEHICLES. THE
BOOM WAS MADE OF
TUBE STEEL WELDED
TOGETHER IN JACK'S
OWN SPECIAL WAY.

BUT IT HAD A LITTLE
PROBLEM; THE FRONT
END WOULD LIFT UP LIKE
A GIANT TEETER-TOTTER.
BUT JACK WOULD FIX
THAT BY HAVING HIS
EXTRA-LARGE PAL
WEIGH IT DOWN.

THE BOOMTRUCK EVENTUALLY ENDED UP ON THE SCRAP HEAP, JUST LIKE THE REST OF THE EXHAUSTED VEHICLES THAT CAME AND WENT OVER THE YEARS. EVEN OUR BELOVED JUNKYARD DOGS THAT RAN AROUND THE YARD HAD AN EXPIRY DATE.

EVERY CAR THAT JACK OWNED IN HIS LIFETIME HAD TO BE FIXED
SOMEHOW, SO IT WAS A GOOD THING HE HAD A MECHANIC'S LICENCE!
THAT WAS THE FUN PART FOR JACK, THOUGH THE FAMILY DID NOT SHARE
IN HIS FUN. BEFORE EVERY TRIP HE HAD TO REMOVE THE OILY CHAINS,
WRENCHES, SPARE PARTS, ETC. FROM THE CAR BEFORE WE COULD SIT
DOWN. THIS RITUAL WOULD TAKE ABOUT HALF AN HOUR, BUT WHEN WE
FINALLY GOT IN THE CAR, OF COURSE, IT WOULDN'T START!

OVER THE YEARS THE CARS
STACKED UP LIKE CORDWOOD, AND
WHEN THERE WAS NO MORE ROOM
IN THE YARD IT WAS TIME TO HAUL
HIS WEALTH DOWN TO THE WAXMAN
SCRAP COMPANY IN HAMILTON.

THERE, THEY'D BE CRUSHED
INTO CUBES THE SIZE OF HAY BALES,
THEN SENT TO EITHER THE STELCO
OR DOFASCO STEEL MILLS WHERE
THEY'D BE MELTED DOWN INTO RAW
METAL. THE RECYCLING PROCESS
WOULD START AGAIN, AND THE METAL
WOULD BECOME SOMETHING NEW!

JACK NEVER REALLY RETIRED FROM THE SCRAP METAL BUSINESS, BUT IN HIS '70S HE DID SLOW DOWN... MOSTLY. THE YARD STILL ATTRACTED SCRAP, LIKE AN OLD TRACTOR HE GOT FROM A FARMER ONE TIME. JACK THOUGHT THAT WAS GREAT, BECAUSE IT REPLACED THE BOOMTRUCK, "IN A WAY."

HE EVEN USED IT TO SAW WOOD, BY LOOPING A LONG BELT FROM THE TRACTOR TO THE SAW TABLE. ONLY JACK KNEW HOW TO WORK THE THING, AND HE HAD TO REASSURE MY BROTHER THAT "THE OPERATOR IS IN CONTROL."

HE HAD ANOTHER SAW TOO, BUT THAT ONE WAS FOR PLAYING MUSIC.

ONE THING JACK DID NOT WANT TO BE RECYCLED WAS
AN OLD SCHOOL BUS, WHICH HE USED AS A WORKSHOP FOR
MAKING TOYS FOR HIS GRANDKIDS. ITS WHEELS DIDN'T GO
ROUND AND ROUND ANYMORE, BUT THE BUS WAS LOTS
OF FUN FOR THE KIDS TO PLAY HIDE AND SEEK IN,
AND EVENTUALLY IT TOO WAS RECYCLED.

THE YEARS ROLLED ON, AND JACK
FINALLY HAD TO GIVE UP HIS DRIVER'S
LICENCE, WHICH WAS TOUGH ON HIM.
VEHICLES WERE IN HIS BLOOD, AS
WAS THE GAS HE'D SIPHONED
OVER THE YEARS.

NOW IN HIS NINETIES, THE ONLY
THING HE COULD LEGALLY DRIVE
WAS A SCOOTER. BUT HE WAS
DELIGHTED TO HAVE WHEELS AGAIN,
AND COULDN'T WAIT TO SHOW OFF,
DOING 'DONUTS' FOR ANYONE
WHO MIGHT BE WATCHING.

MOST DAYS JACK WOULD CRUISE
THE YARD, WHICH BY NOW WAS A PILE
OF HALF-BURIED SCRAP METAL JUST
WAITING FOR TREASURE-HUNTERS
TO DISCOVER. HE WOULD BRING
WHATEVER TREASURES HE FOUND
HOME, PROUD AS PUNCH THAT
HE WAS BACK IN BUSINESS
ONCE AGAIN.

NOW AND THEN JACK WOULD STRAY FROM THE YARD. SOMETIMES HE WOULD PICK VEGETABLES AND SWAP THEM WITH THE NEIGHBOURS FOR BAKED GOODS, MUCH TO EMILY'S DELIGHT. THERE WERE TIMES HE HEADED DOWN TO THE CORNER STORE FOR CANDY OR ICE CREAM. "I SCREAM, YOU SCREAM, WE ALL SCREAM FOR ICE CREAM!" HE WOULD YELL.

SOMETIMES THE POLICE WOULD BRING JACK HOME, EXPLAINING THAT HIS SCOOTER DEFINITELY WASN'T ROADWORTHY. BUT NEXT DAY HE'D BE BACK ON THE ROAD AGAIN. NO-ONE WAS GOING TO TELL JACK WHAT TO DO, AND HE USUALLY GOT AWAY WITH IT, SINCE EVERYONE FIGURED HE'D FORGOTTEN THE RULES ON ACCOUNT OF HIS AGE.

'SCRAPPY JACK' THORNBORROW, 1906-2006

THIS BIOGRAPHY OF MY FATHER 'SCRAPPY JACK' THORNBORROW WAS ORIGINALLY WRITTEN AND ILLUSTRATED FOR HIS 100TH BIRTHDAY IN 2006. ALL THE STORIES ARE BASED ON REAL-LIFE EXPERIENCES JACK HAD TOLD ME ABOUT OVER THE YEARS, WHILE I WAS GROWING UP. HE WAS HARD-WORKING AND PLAYFUL, A SALT-OF-THE-EARTH KIND OF GUY, WHO HAD HIS OWN WAY OF DOING THINGS.

THE CYCLE OF LIFE, AS REPRESENTED BY WHEELS, BECAME A THEME FOR ME TO TELL JACK'S STORIES. FOR A HUNDRED YEARS, FROM HIS CHILDHOOD, THROUGH THE DECADES INTO ADULTHOOD, HE KEPT HIS PLAYFULNESS AND NEVER ACTED HIS AGE!

I DEDICATE THIS BOOK TO JACK, AND TO MY MOM EMILY, WHO ENDURED HIS ANTICS OVER THE YEARS.

WRITTEN AND ILLUSTRATED BY JOAN STEACY

JOAN STEACY GREW UP IN SOUTHERN ONTARIO, AND IS A GRADUATE OF SHERIDAN COLLEGE, THE ONTARIO COLLEGE OF ART & DESIGN UNIVERSITY, AND THE UNIVERSITY OF VICTORIA. WITH HER HUSBAND KEN STEACY SHE CO-CREATED THE COMICS AND GRAPHIC NOVELS PROGRAM AT CAMOSUN COLLEGE IN VICTORIA, BC, WHERE SHE TAUGHT FROM 2012 TO 2020.

HER FIRST GRAPHIC NOVEL *AURORA BOREALICE: A GRAPHIC MEMOIR,* WAS PUBLISHED BY CONUNDRUM PRESS IN 2019, AND WAS LISTED AS ONE OF "TEN CANADIAN COMICS TO READ RIGHT NOW" BY THE CBC, WINNING THE SEQUENTIAL MAGAZINE AWARD FOR BEST GRAPHIC NOVEL OF 2019. JOAN ALSO PRODUCED THE ILLUSTRATIONS FOR A BIOGRAPHY OF OUR GREATEST CANADIAN, TITLED "A BOY NAMED TOMMY DOUGLAS" WHICH IS PUBLISHED BY MIDTOWN PRESS AS WELL.

WWW.JOANSTEACY.COM
JOANSTEACY.BLOGSPOT.COM